the boundaries of return

the boundaries of return

———

poems by
SCOTT ANDREW CHRISTENSEN

R·H·B

First published in the United Kingdom
This edition published 2014 by Red Hand Books

RED HAND BOOKS
Old Bath Road, London SL3 0NS
1618 Yishan Road, Minhang District, 201103 Shanghai
150th Avenue, Springfield Gardens, 11413 New York
Şerifali Mahallesi, Umraniye 34775 Istanbul
Cross Road A, Andheri, 400093 Mumbai

www.rhbks.com

ISBN: 978-1-910346-00-6 (Paperback)
ISBN: 978-1-910346-01-3 (Hardback)

Copyright © 2014 by Scott Andrew Christensen

The right of Scott Andrew Christensen to be identified as the author of this work has been asserted by him in accordance with the Copyrights, Designs and Patents Act of 1988.

This book is sold subject to the condition that it shall not, by way of trade or otherwise, be lent, re-sold, hired out, or otherwise circulated without the publisher's prior consent in any form of binding or cover other than that in which it is published and without a similar condition including this condition being imposed on the subsequent purchaser.

ACKNOWLEDGEMENTS
The author is grateful to the editors of the following magazines where some of these poems first appeared: *The Comstock Review, Contemporary Verse 2, The Dalhousie Review, The Fiddlehead, Prism International,* and *Poetry Salzburg Review.*

Printed and bound in the United Kingdom.

the boundaries of return

CONTENTS

natural features

1.	unsure	*11*
2.	at the glacier	*12*
3.	of tuckamore	*13*
4.	istanbul	*15*
5.	polish the sinew	*16*
6.	the climate of water	*17*
7.	at the narrows	*18*
8.	saddled branches	*19*
9.	ask for more water	*20*
10.	the misery of reconciliation	*21*
11.	creation	*22*
12.	chores to do	*23*
13.	athens, april	*24*
14.	it's too quiet here	*25*

fauna, flora

1.	the foxes	*29*
2.	of beautiful heat	*30*
3.	soothing the sapling	*31*
4.	lichen	*32*
5.	reach for the robin's toe	*33*
6.	robins, here	*34*
7.	as though everyone were watching	*35*
8.	the thimble-sparrow	*36*
9.	before the butterfly	*37*
10.	fahrenheit	*38*
11.	the boundaries of return	*39*

12.	catching the morning	40
13.	caribou at night	41
14.	buckets of buffed caw	42
15.	arbitrary august	43
16.	the moths	44
17.	awaiting the wolf bite	45
18.	rain (and river eddies)	46
19.	the colour of tea	47
20.	seeds of language	48

in the distant reach

1.	the things we like to do	53
2.	firmer angles	54
3.	garlic mashed potatoes	55
4.	today they took hatay teyze	56
5.	bottle-necked at the key-hole	57
6.	in the distant reach	58
7.	the fears of others	59
8.	far from the furrow	60
9.	husks of fallow seeds	61
10.	cracked as an iceberg	63
11.	seeds pocketing the rain	64

about the author   67

natural features

unsure
―――

unsure
of what to call
his new shed,
dad painted
the chipboard walls
in big, square letters.

sometimes
you just can't
name things quickly.
or, in fits of fairness,
creations
become their surroundings.
bird offers a feather
dipping into the unknown,
boughs reach
to taste
my father's brush.

ignoring the rake
its glances headlong
through the
unfinished window,
leaves distil colours
and fall,
envious of spring.

at the glacier
―――

      words
        come and go
          like a valley
            of corresponding dreams.

      at the glacier—
        or lucidity
          of a lake—

        visions
          twist and turn
          towards
          another
        altitude,
          to
        the ripe knowing.

            the river
            rescues
            bedded rock
            from answers,
            cradles
            quarried questions
            to
            the understanding delta.

of tuckamore
―――

i miss
the desert flowers
in november,
forty-five nights
from fond september
and
the rains
of a new year.

my home-born seeds
—tight fingers, aching roots—
whisper to me
    outside
  the further-land
      of
        morning tuckamore
          and
              mire muskeg.

here
the sand is cement,
netherly
sat-upon shores,
and fodder
for salty sidewalks.
here
the sun is
ne'er as warm, drowning
with licking glances
between
knuckled dwarf pine.

this further-land—
    vanilla
        ice cream acres—
    thirsty layers
        soon spring.

istanbul
(serving messages of water)

say something
about istanbul.
  frisk
    the
      fish
      from
        commitments,
      they are
    sesame seeds
      surviving
        the edible day.

fragrance
commends
  constantinople.
    spices
  finger
    aroma,
      serve
        the messages
        of water.

  fighting
  for
    simit
  tossed like circus
  into
      competing wakes,
        seagulls
      court ferries.
      currents
        return,
      taste docks,
        envy sky.

polish the sinew
(*dhahran to ras tanura*)
———

        where are people
           buried?
        the sand searches
          for signs of decay.
     between here, and the seas
         (the pair of them,
          with their gulfs),
      wind reminds water
            to be persistent.

how can a dune
hold handshakes
  —a glove for roots—
    when
it cannot decide
      how many fingers it has?

      can't grip
     the gravestone,
       only grab bones
          and polish the sinew
         to dislocated dust.

the climate of water
―――

i'm so close
to sad, the
  tentacles,
   their tease,
i taste the
    surface
   they promote,
the authorship
of angst
  underneath.

as though
 a *carrefour*
   of sand
    salt,
   wave and wind,
   or
its finer accomplishments,
as though
  it could consider
anything sorrow.

    could arrest
   the dangling atrophy,
  the fine ink
 at odds
in
  the climate of water.

at the narrows
———

headlong
through the narrows
like dice
departing the fist
a dory
shakes hands
with blind waves
ripe among the resistance.

the ballast
finds feet uncomfortable,
and pushes back
at the transom,
straightening his arms.

the oar obeys
the gull-song, her
warning
whisked to further rocks—
the gale's stomach
filled with potatoes,
apples,
axe handles and pitchforks
capsized
at the narrows.

                              saddled branches
                              ―――

    signaled
     by
      a
   local gust
    the
     locust
preens his mandibles
    as though
     the
      breeze
       were
        some
         symbolic gesture.

    as if
     the day
     could sleep
      without night,
    as if
     the tree
      could
    convince its leaves
     otherwise.

branches saddled
by multiple spurs,
    abdomens
     twitch
      to the
       unsung
       hum
      of
        a gathering
      twister.

ask for more water
(sharing shade pt. i)
―――

    when the fruit trees
    find enough gall
    to ask
    for more water, *üssün bey*
    complies, ushers dusk
    from the nethers
    in full accomplice.

    how can we feed you?
    they ask in a chorus
    of good will,
    when you don't feed us?
    waiting with the patience
    of the village
    prayer call, they huddle,
    leaves like palms.

    drinking together, and
    discussing
    the preciousness of water
    they mull why
    the minaret has no branches.
    they decide it drinks
    direct from clouds,
    that blossoms
    are not always necessary
    to beckon rain.

the misery of reconciliation

behemoth
comes from the
    hebrew,
anything very large
and powerful.

my daughter
wouldn't understand
the immensity,
sitting here,
spilled orange juice and grapes
the colour of crayons
snug to the palm
and its pulling fingers.

    i met a woman
    from tel aviv
    her greek friend said
    "writers are born."

she—the athenian—should
see my little monster
borderless scribbling, now
the tv
a portrait of missiles,
creation
searching for
the misery of reconciliation.

creation
(come the wind)
___

        the wind—
        in repeated gestures
        of breath,
          as though
           the baby
          were to be born
             here,
               party to my tea—
seizes the scold
from
my beverage
and returns, tepid
tasting the innocent vapour
in all its
pushing humidity.

last year, here
at the cabin door
we winked
warning waves
in rolling admiration,
in gardens
of sweet arrival,
in furrows
of
faint breezes.

chores to do
(sharing shade pt. ii)
———

this morning,
with the coffee
there are chores to do,
including a list
of the things
i should have said.

but
flowers remember
the garden, and
waves
claw for my ear.
the words escapade
like mice mocking
the trap—
cheddar laments purpose,
dries in crumbly loss
impaled under appliances.

the hose limp,
would it matter
if i didn't water
the morning light?
in ranging bougainvillea
the sea continues
to offer advice,
tasting my coffee
with unknown answers,
seasoning soup
with the salty breath
of the unsaid.

athens, april
―――

    4am to the pharmacy
    a patina gloves the moon
    in fresh responsibility.

    the taxi
    tricks shadows
    into a game
    of hide-and-seek,
    streetlights compete
    with
    the chasing illumination.

    the hotel room
    murmurs in malcontent
    for its missing,
    windows caress the street
    for father's kiss.

it's too quiet, here
(sharing shade pt. iii)
———

i can hear
god thinking,
the cricket
sprinkles rosin.
moon yawns,
a scythe
swooping sharp
for september, for
forage, and
decisions full of fallow.

then, navigating a
tractor tire track—
befriending manure,
tired of the symphony—
cricket retires
to the other side of the road,
and the ditch
that drowns decibels.

she doesn't know
how different
the water tastes,
how she sounds
under the surface
of so many stars
reckless with silence.

fauna, flora

                    the foxes
(for semra and simon on the hill)

the foxes
  in and out
    of the pine.

why does the
  hilltop exhale
    their
      footprints,
why does
  snow exhibit
  the extremities
    of silence?

can they see
  the contour
  of the
    fragrant planting,
does
  the window
    offer the chance
  to remember.

of beautiful heat
———

        by a choir
          of beautiful heat
            rain whistles, and
robes catch the tireless echo,
          the endless
            shuffle of embers.

      the fox remains
        aloof
to any indiscretions,
        answering the fire
          with its ears
        as
    the pine sap sings,
        hisses
at the matchstick
        and its magic.

                              soothing the sapling
                              ───

buffalo dead
   in the frozen lake
      where are the mallards,
         their wagging tails?
      will the ice be broken
         by wings, hovering
            at the throat of the river?

         how soon salmon
            will inherit the strength
               of the water's rage.
            the animals, feet wet,
               their need for movement
                  like wind.

                     the submerged paddle
                   whispers at winter,
                        reciting reed-song,

                   soothing the sapling.

lichen
(going to the market)
———

        lichen absorbs
        the warming.

        barking in
        the gist
        of another curb,
        another collar
        hot
        at the
        phaeton's phantom.

        its fixations
        flirting, asserting
        the
        terminal firth.

        to the final
        thirst,
        the lapping streets
        of
        renewed
        resuscitation.

                    reach for the robin's toe
                  (twenty minutes on a rooftop)

wind, breath of mine,
hallelujah
of the high pine,
your sweeping skirt hem
blouse between boughs
murmuring leaves
wave to your twirling whimsy.

    hands, they are
    these leaves—
    clapping
    , and
    reach
    for the robin's toe
    waltz on this arm
    amid musical air—

sway, my stormy hemlock
drop your hands, october hardwood
see the pleat gather
sweet maple, your clouds
counting sigh-steps
atop the timid trees.

robins, here

        the robin, here
        has been washed
        of his crayola
            breast.
              unbuttoned
           to
         an
        ashen undercoat,
        hopping
        sky to that sky,
        she serves invisibility.

        where did you swim
        my adept crooner
        to christen
        this unusual vest?

          expect
         the beak
          to burst
            back
        to the nostrils,
          a mask
         of pencil yellow
        nibbling at notes
        newfound
        at my nerves.

                no worms
                service the sand
                here, palms
                provide perches.

as though everyone were watching
(something about alice st. elementary)

the birds forget
i can smell them
as they hop
in arcing consultation
to the next lonely branch.

their feathers
reminiscent of kindergarten,
   —the cat too quick—
   prancing, she carries
   the sparrow at the abdomen
   as though everyone were watching.

their call
flowers near the schoolyard
   —the janitor buries things there—
   tombstones bowled over
   the earth holding
   tiny stolen pipe cleaner crosses.

and in the grass
robins emanate sky,
upon return lift the layer
of cool isolation
from
the backyard snow.

the thimble-sparrow
———

        headfirst, into
        the
        harsh window
        like a hammer (i think)
        the thimble-sparrow
        in splayed spill
        below
        the
        broken tea-cup
        of this, the
        roman theatre
        thought
        the murderous mirror
        the uncourteous curtain
        oh! ungracious glass

            the
            falling
            façade,
            the
                other side
           of
                herself

before the butterfly

a blade of grass
tempts the cricket
with decision. *this
is my beautiful neck,*
she confides
in the beckoning,
*the photographer wants us
before the butterfly.*

framed, a bird in a tree
contemplates her approach,
the taste of cricket.
days document the urgency
like a shutter, the
snap and release
of a moment
pulled onto a spool,
teasing the future.

dusk finds forfeit
into recollection
and the appetite
of memory. grass
grins, bird interrupts
her hunger.

fahrenheit
(sharing shade pt. v)
_____

        doors close
        a key
        combs the heat.
        follicles fear
        freckles will drown
        from incessant irrigation.

        the olive, the
        vine
        ripen the breeze
        between garden greetings,
        wait for bird wing
        to shuffle shade.

        blossoms taste
        the sparrow heel.
        tempting feathers
        with messages from bees,
        they measure the coolness
        of unwritten birdsong.

the boundaries of return

i guess
the nasturtiums
will miss us most,
rising to
an unknown occasion,
challenging the
    peach tree
to greater circumstances.

even the gulls
garnish departures
in showering dare,
the way hands
harbor excursion
in flight, admiration
    and the
        non-forgetting.

if we plant
the *malta erik*
before the remaining
pines burst,
will it
blossom
under the boundaries
    of return?

catching the morning
―

    catching the morning's sky
    wet
    with burled knots
    caramel, and
    lofty wisps of
    butterscotch

    the owl absorbs
    pinches of light
    falling
    to the forest floor,
    feathering the breath
    of mice, shrews
    hares tall at the shoulder
    of the pine trunk.

    the fern, the fiddlehead
    open to the owl
    in arcing posture
    lick the tendrils
    of a sugary sky.

caribou at night
without reservations

having greeted the world
lacking a father
my niece's son
adorns himself
with the brave familiarity
of violence.

you can change
your last name—
bludgeoned
until your signature
screams dust.
chew the unwanted word
as you hear it, from
the drum
to the molar,
the sound a canoe
down blind, winding tracts.

at night your namesake
stalked caribou
intent on dreams of murder.
so many weapons
airborne, and
filled with the silence
of thunder, of bones
and new habits
under cowering rain,
fists
at the kitchen window.

buckets of buffed caw
———

        the dust corrodes
         t h e   e
                  s   a
      as though
     asked
       by the
         sardine saline
        to
     prepare a mustard,
     a kind of

          d a r d a n elle-ic
           dressing
           of
          d ee per
          fa
            t hom
             i
            cal
          saff
          ron.

served by the
pine-birds
and their
buckets
of
buffed caw,
wind
whisks
in constant satiation.

arbitrary august
waiting for hakam

---

cormorants
crack smiles
from
guileless lips, the
    ones
  they use
to whistle at fish,
      beneath ballast below
    bowsprits
               in
  the constant coming.

in the reclamation
of returning
seabirds sing
on my tidal prairie,
the intimate aftermath
of certain acknowledgments.

because swimming
is a gift
reserved for those
without fin,   for those
     fishing
   in the forgetfulness,
  angling in another
arbitrary august.

the moths

    the moths
    of invention
      twitter about

        nightlights
      in caressful
       frosting—
    don't come in here
      for
        i'll
      turn off
        the light!

and scatter
all the thoughts
you've been
      preventing.

awaiting the wolf bite
(just beyond beypazarı)
———

my knee dirty
from dropping
to take a picture,
dogs lap
the hues of shade,
sleep
in forged collars
from the blacksmith.

the shepherd
swims from the lens, says
*someone bought one hundred
but i haven't been paid*
awaits
the wolf bite,
son returning from lunch.

my hovering hand
guesses the age
he opened his mouth
to the hills,
soon he will take
the remainder
up to trees where
the sun paints shadows
in random mysteries,
shifting
in the light
of the day's greeting,
where trunks hide teeth
full of illumination.

rain (and river eddies)
george daydreams in swedish

reaching half-wrist
cocks and pulls
the prize
to the surface.
how much water
will glove my hand
after gravity grabs
the garment
from my fingers?

tide to the tips
of the estuary
keeps dreams
of delicious rain
expectant.
the river eddy
kisses my palm,
from the trout's tail
a wave of salutation.

the current
offers refuge
to its own. diving
back to the surface
arm extended,
gills rasp
at the tethered fly,
eyes comparing novelty.

the colour of tea
beypazarı bayram
———

    the butterfly

        light

      as

    mind's
      linger

    anoints
another head,
      hard to the sun,   the
            flickering
          heat.

petals applaud
the
insistence of rain.

the colour
  of tea
    sends
  each reaching stick
      and
        terrible
      stone
    collecting, colliding
    at
the roadside graves.

seeds of language
(for george upon listening to bowie's "conversation piece")
namesake part one
―――

                where does
                  the sand
               pretend to know
          your name, scattered like
            seeds of language
              melting dust
                in troughs
              of descending.

                at the base
             of the mountain
             the bird speaks
            tongues of song
            perched on peaks
        where rocks murmur,
dreaming of disintegration.

and, when
the tree speaks

speak, tree
now
speak
he is gone. quiet

tree
walks and
elaborates, some
small
bird
  l i s t e n s

throughout the naming—
whether whispers at the cheek,
or wind
quiet as clouds
at the canyon—
sand settles
in the echo in the rhythm
of new sounds.

in the distant reach
———

the things we like to do
for george messo

and when
he went fishing
his mind—
car casting by all the minarets
and
unremarkable roads
like light on water—
the sky swarmed
with questions
unequalled in their
ability to lure answers.

the bait—
as though bored,
or given to
some other bird
or animal
in equal query—
offered itself
in swollen pieces,
in the requisite measure
of
the things we like to do.

and the line
answered back,
as though a telephone call
from some depth
where light remembers.

firmer angles
l'existence première partie
———

    how can
    supple
    be found in *supplemental*
    as if a wrist, a
    rising thigh
    an ankle open
    to the frightened sea
    could be anything *extra*?

    strands
    streamline the neck,
    singing in the
    hand's fantasy,
    curling deeper into the
    collarbone cups.

    further, the descent
    fingers taut ribs
    and pelvic ears,
    two open palms
    in offering elevation
    at the cinched waist.

    yes—the thigh,
    still ascending
    brings the back of the knee
    to firm angles,
    to the chagrin
    collecting distant shorebirds.

garlic mashed potatoes
———

i can't smell
   the garlic mashed potatoes
   the way
     my colleagues can.

fresh from the microwave
   they congregate,
     the lunch room
       a chance
      for different types of questions.

and
i remember *smell*
   is the first sense
    to falter
      when hosting alzheimer's
       (what did
        father say,
          the farm—
            fire—
        the potatoes melting
        like memories
          inside the flame?)

is there
 another way
    to see transgressions,
    see them
   before they are forgotten?

my lunch frowns
at the thought
of forgiveness.

today they took hatay teyze
___

       today
       they took
       hatay teyze to
            the *hastane*—
            how fast is the fast boat?
            as if
            the seagulls
            could find her, now
            as if
the islands
            could withstand her absence?

the *istavrit*,
levrek
melting in her son's hands

gills guiding
the length of the unlikely sea.

bottle-necked at the key-hole
(dans la bateau)
———

littering
the floor
with the snippets
of sun
in constant crisis
in strict parlay
wedging open
the slats
of your ferry seat
the waiting
the insidious knock
of brilliance,
their cadence
bottle-necked
at
the key-hole.

in the distant reach
―――

        perhaps
        there is a planet
        with my name
        circling in echo
        somewhere else.

        for instance:
                a body of rocks
                held together
                in adherence
                to a new element—
                singing
                a new note—
                somewhere off
                the unattainable charts.

        finding membership
        in the distant reach
        of raised voices,
        belonging
        to the purpose,
        the atmosphere of music.

        ice bubbles
        absorbing the sun
        tiny unknown planets.

the fears of others

i renamed
the file
"mom's release"
and chuckled out loud
at the dislocation,
at the distance
of remembering.

the house is gone, now.
the bedroom floor,
just before
it was sold,
its linoleum—
all out of sorts
waiting for me
to come crashing down,
again, this time
from
the emptying attic—
fought with its geometry,
with the art
of full circle.

burned with her blood
at my appearance
it now supports
the fears of others.

far from the furrow
———

       well,
           hallelujah!
       and whatever else
       you wanted to tell me.

       your cigarette defies logic,
       your hair
       another outcome.

       prancing in the square
       i thought you'd never die.
       so many of our friends
       impotent
       like seeds
       packaged far from the furrow,
       you splashed them
       from the fountain
       as if you knew
       they'd take root.

       the waist cinched,
           brown skirt
       open to your mouth
       lips frisk the smoke
       for your exaltations,
       and whatever else
       you wanted to say.

husks of fallow seeds
(prologue to a new york pen)

found:
substantial pen,
writes well.
some torn words.
seen grounded
like birdseed.
ink murmurs,
husks of fallow grain
falling from a fist.

i have a pen
from nasd, where
northwest of wall street
we served bagels
and
fresh orange juice, coffee
from pumping urns
high above ground zero.

when the tray
carrying cakes and cookies
found the boardroom
i slipped that pen
into the pocket
of my black bistro apron,
stealing a moment
from
the less infamous
heights of manhattan.

the night before
it rained. and then people
caught paper
caressing the sky
in fingering consolation.

lost:
ability to feel.
chance to find shadows
as appealing alternatives.
lightness of footsteps
in the dust
of loss.

cracked as an iceberg
———

in this unsung
and irregular profession,
you must engage
the cold coffee.

hot as some words
may be,
in their
incomplete forging—
drowning
in the cool
      sparkling
           confession—

the mug carries on,
cracked as an iceberg,
bleeding
from the avalanche.

seeds pocketing the rain
(seeds pt. iii)
———

but, if
there are no seeds
to pocket the rain,
how can the desert
create her poetry?

like sweet compost
fragrant syllables insist
in thirsty layers
on sprouting skyward,
of creating hubris.
water cans
cast the cadence
of captured rain.

calling rapture, words
reach,
a kite shrugs
its pointed shoulders
at the blanketing butterscotch
and its constant ripple.

spring tendrils
in fresh ache
pluck the arcing string.
the tether billows
in broad gestures,
wind orchestrates
the swell of husks
unbuttoning,
applauds
latent rain.

about the author
———

SCOTT ANDREW CHRISTENSEN was born in Truro, Nova Scotia, and now lives in the Middle East with his wife and two daughters. He completed an MFA in English & Writing from Southampton College, Long Island University. He has published poetry in *The Comstock Review*, *Contemporary Verse 2*, *The Dalhousie Review*, *The Fiddlehead*, *Prism International* and *Poetry Salzburg Review*, among others. His R·H·B title, *the boundaries of return*, is his first collection of poems. He also writes fiction.

www.rhbks.com

www.ingramcontent.com/pod-product-compliance
Lightning Source LLC
Chambersburg PA
CBHW031422040426
42444CB00005B/682